Collins

Cherry Blossoms

Rhymes and Stories

Nursery

FS1

SERIES EDITOR: RANI THIPPAVAZZULA

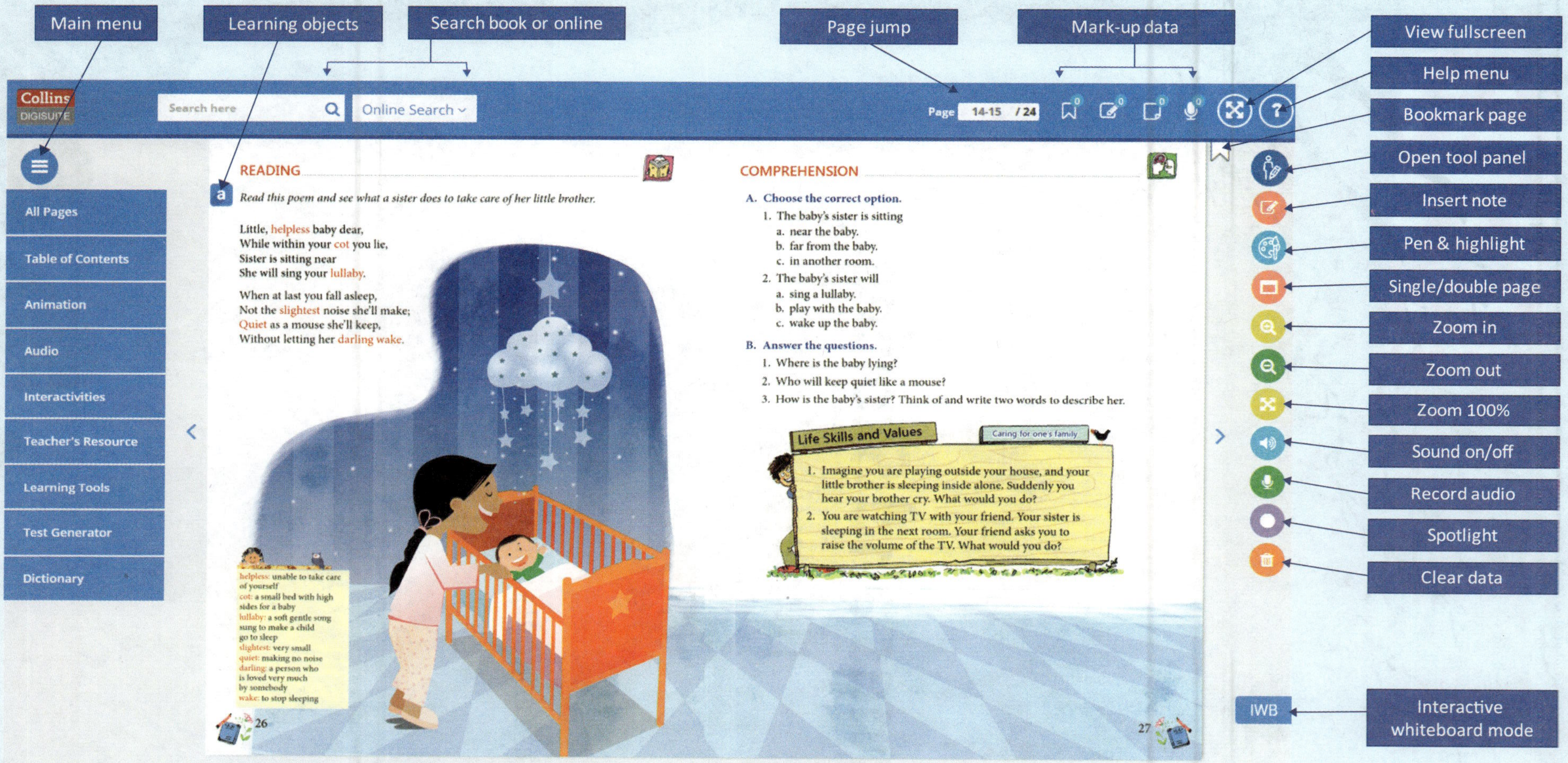

Student + Teacher			Teacher-only	
a animations	**ia** activities	**g** games	**lp** lesson plans	**tn** teacher's notes
ilt instructor-led tutorials	**w** worksheets	**v** videos	**w** worksheets	**ak** answer keys
	audio			

Preface

Cherry Blossoms provides graded, age-appropriate learning opportunities targeting holistic skill development for children in the age group of 3 years to 8 years. The series aligns with the vision outlined in the National Education Policy, 2020 for early years. It spreads across five levels, Nursery (Foundational Stage 1) to Class 2 (Foundational Stage 5). The books use a combination of hands-on activities, frequent recapitulation and child-friendly artwork to facilitate learning.

The series comprises **40 books** and spans **English**, **Maths**, **General Awareness**, and **Art and Craft**. The series comes bundled with a **workbook** for each subject and a book of **rhymes** and **stories** for Foundational Stage 1 to 3.

This series integrates the essence of **NIPUN Bharat** guidelines, which extensively deal with Foundational Literacy and Numeracy. The series aims to motivate learners to read independently, to improve their vocabulary, number sense and spatial understanding. The **Foundational Literacy and Numeracy (FLN)** skills include the skills for developing their critical thinking, logical reasoning and creative skills, as well as the skills to enhance their ability to express themselves both verbally and in writing.

Cherry Blossoms Teacher Support Materials include:

Teacher's Resource Books: Comprises stories, activity banks, classroom management and assessment guidelines

Multimedia eBook: Consists of animations, audio, video, slide shows, and interactive exercises

Print-ready Worksheets: Additional worksheets for practice and reinforcement, present in the digital support

Digital Flashcards: Flashcards with embedded sounds and animations for letter formation and letter-sound association

Animations and Songs: Animated stories and rhymes set to tune

Interactive Games: Interactivities to reinforce concepts in a fun and engaging manner

A note on the activity banks (included in the Teacher's Manuals)

The activity banks comprise hands-on activities that will help children develop the requisite skills to attain age-appropriate learning goals. In keeping with Howard Gardener's theory of multiple intelligences, the activity banks include options and variations that enable teachers to provide a planned cycle of experiences and opportunities, which foster each type of intelligence, to every child in their classrooms. The activity banks equip teachers to use the strengths of children as a means of complementing their less developed areas by valuing and nurturing the inherent abilities of the children.

Rani Thippavazzula, former Academic Director, Ravindra Bharathi Group is an eminent educationist with over two decades of experience in teaching, administration and curriculum design and development. As an Academic Advisor for chain schools pan India, she is proficient in developing learning products and is a specialist in Differentiated Instruction, Enterprise Education and Early Childhood Education.

Learning and Development During the Early Years

The early years are the most significant years for growth, development and learning. During this period, children need adequate opportunities for stimulating experiences as these favourably affect various learning abilities. Learning experiences, when chosen and planned properly, fuel the innate curiosity of children, and stimulate their thought processes.

The goal of learning during the early years is to enhance the all-round development of personality and to inculcate healthy attitudes, life skills and good values. Creative play, well thought-out games and developmentally appropriate activities help children develop the necessary skills to achieve these goals. The skills that children need to acquire can broadly be categorized as:

Motor:
Motor skills pertain not only to gross motor activities like walking and jumping but also include fine motor activities like the ability to hold a pencil and write. The development of motor skills is facilitated through several graded activities.

Personal, Social and Emotional:
Personal, social and emotional development, necessary for the overall personality development of children, is achieved using a combination of hands-on activities, role plays and thought-provoking stories and rhymes.

Linguistic:
The ability to listen, speak, read and write is critical to success in formal learning environments.

Mathematical:
The development of mathematical ideas and concepts is important at this stage since children will continue to build on this learning for most of their years of schooling.

Knowledge and Understanding of the World:
This is achieved through activities that enable children to explore their surroundings at home and in the school, and interact with the people that they see around them.

Health and Safety: The idea of health and safety is introduced through activities, stories and retelling of real-life experiences to encourage children to focus on health and well-being.

Creative:
Creative skills are developed through a host of activities involving art, craft, painting, roleplays, etc.

Logical and Rational Thinking:
Activities that involve simple puzzles, pattern-completion and visual discrimination help children to develop logical and rational thinking skills.

Contents

CHUBBY CHEEKS, DIMPLE CHIN

Chubby cheeks, dimple chin,
Rosy lips, teeth within,
Curly hair, very fair,
Eyes are blue, lovely too,
Teacher's pet, is that you?
Yes, Yes, Yes!

JOHNNY, JOHNNY

Johnny, Johnny,
Yes, Papa!
Eating sugar?
No, Papa!
Telling lies?
No, Papa!
Open your mouth.
Ha! Ha! Ha!

HOP A LITTLE, JUMP A LITTLE

Hop a little, jump a little,
One, two, three.
Run a little, skip a little,
Tap one knee.
Bend a little, stretch a little,
Nod your head.
Yawn a little, sleep a little,
In your bed.

BAA, BAA, BLACK SHEEP

Baa, baa, black sheep,
Have you any wool?
Yes, sir! Yes, sir!
Three bags full.
One for the master,
And one for the dame,
And one for the little boy
Who lives down the lane.

TWO LITTLE HANDS

Two little hands go clap, clap, clap,
Two little feet go tap, tap, tap,
Two little eyes are open wide,
One little head goes side to side.

ONE, TWO, BUCKLE MY SHOE

One, two,
Buckle my shoe.

Three, four,
Shut the door.

Five, six,
Pick up sticks.

Seven, eight,
Lay them straight.

Nine, ten,
A big, fat hen.

TWO LITTLE DICKIE BIRDS

Two little dickie birds sitting on a wall.
One named Peter, one named Paul.
Fly away, Peter! Fly away, Paul!
Come back, Peter! Come back, Paul!

RAIN, RAIN, GO AWAY

Rain, rain, go away,
Come again another day.
Little Johnny wants to play.
Rain, rain, go away.

TWINKLE, TWINKLE, LITTLE STAR

Twinkle, twinkle, little star,
How I wonder what you are!
Up above the world so high,
Like a diamond in the sky!

EENY, MEENY, MINY, MOE

Eeny, meeny, miny, moe,
Catch a tiger by the toe.
If he hollers, let him go,
Eeny, meeny, miny, moe.

HUMPTY DUMPTY

Humpty dumpty sat on a wall.
Humpty dumpty had a great fall.
All the King's horses
And all the King's men
Could not put Humpty together again.

RUB-A-DUB-DUB

Rub-a-dub-dub,
Three men in a tub,
And who do you think they be?
The butcher, the baker, the candlestick maker,
And all of them out to sea.

HOT CROSS BUNS!

Hot cross buns!
Hot cross buns!
One a penny, two a penny,
Hot cross buns!

If you have no daughters
Give them to your sons.
One a penny, two a penny,
Hot cross buns!

TEDDY BEAR, TEDDY BEAR

Teddy bear, teddy bear,
Turn around!
Teddy bear, teddy bear,
Touch the ground!

Teddy bear, teddy bear,
Jump up high!
Teddy bear, teddy bear,
Touch the sky!

ROW, ROW, ROW YOUR BOAT

Row, row, row your boat,
Gently down the stream.
Merrily, merrily, merrily, merrily,
Life is but a dream.

OLD MACDONALD

Old MacDonald had a farm,
E-I-E-I-O
And on his farm he had a cow,
E-I-E-I-O
With a moo-moo here,
And a moo-moo there,
Here a moo, there a moo,
Everywhere a moo-moo,
Old MacDonald had a farm,
E-I-E-I-O

RING-A-RING O' ROSES

Ring-a-ring o' roses,
A pocket full of posies,
A-tishoo! A-tishoo!
We all fall down.

POLLY PUT THE KETTLE ON

Polly put the kettle on,
Polly put the kettle on,
Polly put the kettle on,
We'll all have tea.
Sukey take it off again,
Sukey take it off again,
Sukey take it off again,
They've all gone away.

TEN LITTLE FINGERS, TEN LITTLE TOES

Ten little fingers, ten little toes,
Two little ears and one little nose,
Two little eyes that shine so bright,
And one little mouth
To kiss mother, goodnight.

EARLY TO BED

Early to bed,
Early to rise,
Makes a man
Healthy, wealthy and wise.

MY SCHOOL BUS

I go to school in a yellow bus.
It has big, round wheels.
It has a LOOOOUUUUDDD horn.
The horn says, "Pom-pom, pom-pom!
Where are you?
The bus is waiting."

Every morning, I jump out of bed.

Mummy gets me ready.
I take my bag and bottle.
"Pom-pom, pom-pom! Where are you?" says the bus.

The door opens.
All my friends greet me.
I kiss mummy.

I get on to the bus.
I am off to school!

JOJO'S DREAM

I am Jojo!
This is my home.
There is a big lake near my home.
There are many flowers too.

I have many friends! We play together.
We splash in the lake together.

There is a big mango tree on the other side of the lake.
It has big, yellow mangoes.
I want to fly to the mango tree.

Mother says it is too far for me. I must become big and strong to reach the mango tree.

So, I practise flying every day with my friends.
I eat the food that mother gives.

One day, I will fly away to the mango tree. I will eat the yellow mangoes. I will get them for my friends too. That is my dream!